PAVED:

Passion, Attitude, Values, Energy, and Determination

The Road to Winning and Success

Dr. Mitchel A. Nickols

A Nickols Worth Publishing

Tarentum, Pennsylvania

PAVED:
Passion, Attitude, Values, Energy, and Determination

Copyright © 2016 by Dr. Mitchel A. Nickols

A Nickols Worth Publishing
P.O. Box 390
Tarentum, PA 15084
412-944-2643

DrMitchelNickols@gmail.com
www.MoreThanANickolsWorth.com

Printed in the United States of America

Library of Congress Control Number (LCCN): 2016951832

ISBN - 10: 0999404903
ISBN - **13: 9780999404904**

Cover design by: John Robinson II Jrobinson2@gdwoc.org

What We Think

"This book is an essential read and depicts the epitome of how you too can achieve the PAVED life filled with experiential business protocols necessary for business and sustained success. By following the PAVED model of excellence, you too will experience the benefits of success in Business."

—Dr. Howard B. Slaughter, President & CEO, Christian Management Enterprises, LLC Gubernatorial appointee to the Board of the Pennsylvania Economic Development Financing Authority and former Regional Director of Fannie Mae's Southwestern Pennsylvania Business Office

"It is important that the areas focused on in this book have been identified as major factors that lead to the success of individuals not only in the corporate world, but also in life."

—Amos Glenn III, Superintendent, Allegheny Technologies Incorporated

"Working in professional sports takes hard work and dedication. The concepts in PAVED—passion, attitudes, values, energy, determination—can help reinforce characteristics that are critical to success in that and every industry."

—Kimberly Matthews, Human Resources Manager, The Pittsburgh Pirates

"Every great lawyer and business leader, in reflecting on their road to success, can recognize the pertinent role the qualities discussed in PAVED plays in their professional pursuits. The earlier you recognize and reflect on your passion, attitude, values, energy, and determination, the more fulfilling and impactful you will be in your career and life. For those just starting out on their professional journey or for those who have already arrived, understanding and renewing your commitment to these principles is a must for achieving and maintaining your mark in the world."

Two roads diverged in a wood, and I —I took the one less traveled by, And that has made all the difference.

—Robert Frost

Dedication

*In loving memory of my dad and mom,
the late Willie J. Nickols, Jr. and Dr. Bernice Nickols.
They will forever be remembered for their sacrifices and examples of discipline to achieve what you want in life.*

Our attitude controls our lives. Attitudes are a secret power working twenty-four hours a day, for good or bad. It is of paramount importance that we know how to harness and control this great force.

—Irving Berlin

Acknowledgments

Confidence and competence are two of the cornerstones for writing a book. This is not to ignore the compliment of people who either inspired, encouraged, or spent lots of love and time to believe this work would be completed.

First, I must acknowledge my Savior and Lord, and then the woman who has stuck with me as my faithful partner through decades of our journey, Quandra, the love of my life and my best friend. She has served as a bridge at times when I was trying to figure out the next turns that not only impacted my life but that of our whole house. Her patience is immense and her love is unbridled.

Second, I would like to thank my daughters who don't remember all the early years of this journey with their mom and me, but who's unwavering sparkle has always meant a lot to me. It is for Rachelle and Amber that many nights and days were no small task, and their reflective successes are only part of the fruit we enjoy.

Third, all of my supporters in the church and those I have had the privilege of working with professionally and through my college teaching experiences.

Fourth, to my uncle, Dr. Melvin Steals, who sparked my determination to write, which began during one long night when I was an undergraduate student.

And last but not least, to my now 95-year-old mother-in-law, Magnolia Combs, who often nudged me to reach higher.

Goals help you channel your energy into action.

—Les Brown

Foreword

Life is increasingly more demanding, as time can be either our biggest detriment or our biggest asset. High pressure environments keep us distracted. So many of us are so busy multi-tasking that no one thing is done well! This book, by Dr. Mitchel Nickols (PAVED: Passion, Attitude, Values, Energy and Determination) gives us tips to help slow the pace and conserve our energy, while becoming more productive. It can even be transformational if you apply the simple principles.

Dr. Nickols has logged many miles in order to bring this book to fruition. As he looks in the rear-view mirror, he is able to share his wisdom and insights about life and living it to the fullest. One of the most important accomplishments in life is to finish strong, knowing that your life had meaning and impacted others in a positive way. A life with meaning, personally and professionally, is a life worth living. What a legacy!

This book is a compilation by Dr. Nickols who has exemplified a life worth living, a life with a plan and a purpose. The author has faced many crucibles in life and systematically overcame each one. From growing up in a rough neighborhood where many faced incarceration, he internalized his own set of values and used his boundless energy and determination to become a success story. Presently, he is a minister of his own church, an author, a professor, a consultant, husband, father, etc., but more importantly, he's a person of character who truly cares about others and has made a difference in a multitude of peoples' lives.

Well, when I was asked to write this forward for Mitch, I was truly honored! Our lives initially intersected more than a decade ago, as professors and colleagues, teaching at a faith-based university. In our first meeting, we instantly connected. After a brief conversation, we realized that I had taught his daughter in college and she had already shared her positive impressions. The rest is history as they say, as we share many common interests, have collaborated on many projects, encourage and energize each other and most of all, we have FUN!

As you read this book, join Dr. Nickols in his reflection on winning and success. Sit down in a comfortable chair, read, relax and let these principles resonate in your mind. Contemplate, be mindful and think about ways to apply and share these ideas. Maybe, just maybe this book will help pave your future! We clearly need guidance and true inspiration!

Dr. Diane D. Galbraith
Business Professor and Consultant
MBA, Undergraduate Studies and Internships
Slippery Rock University

Table of Contents

Try not to become a man of success but a man of value.

—Albert Einstein

Introduction

If a man is called to be a street sweeper, he should sweep streets even as a Michaelangelo painted, Beethoven composed music or Shakespeare wrote poetry. He should sweep streets so well that all the hosts of heaven and earth will pause to say, 'Here lived a great street sweeper who did his job well.'
                                                                —Martin Luther King Jr.

It would be wishful thinking that we should hold that the current state of things in our lives is just fixed and nothing can be done about them. For most people, there is this phase-driven life that wreaks with possibilities and little clarity about how to get to the next desired stop along the way. Whether you are an expectant mom or a dad with the anticipation of family expansion, much uncertainty abounds. Where should you turn? What should you do next? Or, how do you get to the things your heart is really saying?

My life's journey has been interspersed with people, some professionally prepared, and others who have again and again tried to give life their best shot; those who are in search of not only the next best things, but with questions about their own purpose and how they might fulfill it. Professionally, I have worked with thousands of people in schools, including the college and university level, and other organizations where answers were sought before the right questions were even asked. The road signs in life have pointed people in many directions in attempts to transform their paths. And at the end of each road, not everyone has felt like they have reached their pinnacle.

For nearly 20 years as a graduate school professor, teaching in programs in Organizational Leadership, Community Engagement, and Leadership and Administration, I have witnessed the transformation of a large number of men and women. As a consultant, I have worked with executives (executive leadership training, coaching, and professional development of managerial staffers) who work to improve organizational climate. What has been missing in some of these situations is the importance of self-awareness and how that brings them closer to true transformation.

Dr. Henry Cloud, co-author of the best-selling book, Boundaries, believes that everyone has transformational moments. He outlines what should be considered:

> First, it is the power of people being engaged.
> Second, the power is a force for driving results.
> Third, the power is felt in constant adaptation and learning.
> Fourth, the power is felt in the growth of the people.
> Fifth, the power is felt in the formal motion that is created.
> Finally, the customers and the market feel the power.
> (2013, pp. 45-47)

These wisdom keys spring new vistas in the way we should think about this journey, and not only what meaning it should have for us, but for everyone who goes along for the personal and professional ride.

PAVED represents an acronym that began to develop months ago as I was asked to provide professional development for staff members who had been recognized for their high performance standards statewide and nationally. The lead administrator was concerned that, having received the award, her staff would succumb to lower motivation in the workplace. My attempt was to infuse them with the emergence of Passion, awareness of Attitudes, embracing of core Values, refueling of Energy, and Determination to not only maintain previous gains but to reach for new heights.

The PAVED Model, as I have named it, becomes the basis for helping readers of this book to first discovery or in places, rediscovery of all that matters and returns them to a place which expands their own purpose in life, and how they could enhance the lives of others around them on a regular basis.

Chapter one acquaints each reader with ways to identify their own passion and how to begin a self-awareness and self-nurturing process. Once you identify your passion, you learn how to guard against the things that may derail it. Should this happen, then this book shows you how to refuel your passion again and again. You find those habits that are essential during the refueling process. No car goes without refueling at some point. Critical questions are asked in this chapter to remind you of what you really love doing on a daily basis.

The next chapter grabs your attention by explaining the role of good attitudes and the disdain of bad ones. There are certain things that happen regularly in many workplaces that could affect your attitude. Positive attitude brings positive effects. In this chapter, you learn how to recognize the key characteristics of successful leaders, and regardless of your situation, how to create and maintain a positive attitude.

Chapter three helps you sort through the questions about personal values, core values in the workplace, and the roles those values play in decision-making and effectiveness as a leader. It presents the influential importance of personal value systems and how you might identify your own key values. In this chapter, there is also some discussion about work-life balance, a critical point for leaders whose work and personal life occasionally bleeds outside the lines.

The importance of energy is the focus of chapter four. Even recently, I had a conversation with a top executive in an organization about how to maintain his personal energy level, protect his reserve, and necessary strategies for reasonable dispensing of energy. Key people in homes and the workplace rarely limit what they do to normal working hours. The demands of the job are just that…demands. There is a certain amount of rigor and competence that goes along with being authentic. Maintenance must be put in place with constant checkups. So many things can drain your personal energy and balance must be strongly considered and adhered to. This chapter helps you inventory your personal energy use in meaningful ways.

Chapter five leads you to draw upon both passion and purpose, positive attitudes and values that become your main staples in difficult times. Winning rarely occurs without being stretched and pushed to the limits. Success does not occur unless patterns of drawing on passion and values and an 'I will win no matter what attitude' pans for the energy to make things happen. Certain things become your main ingredients in difficult and challenging times. Those things become a part of your engine and stabilize your navigation system.

Chapter 1
Passion

Every great dream begins with a dreamer. Always remember, you have within you the strength, the patience, and the passion to reach for the stars to change the world.

—Harriet Tubman

A sk anyone if they have dreams, and the response will be different for each person willing to respond. Most people have dreamed at night or while sleeping. The number of dreams remembered will vary from one person to the next. People do not always understand the images, ideas, sensations and emotions associated with their dreams. The same may be true if you ask if they have passion.

Harriet Tubman, noted for her legendary ventures to assist hundreds to successfully flee slavery and plantation living in the south, clearly understood the importance of dreaming and trailblazing, not only for herself, but for others through unenviable travels. She traveled paths that later became roads to freedom. Something on the inside of her would not let her give up.

In an attempt to bring definition to the word passion, Dave Kerpen (2014) in an Inc.com article provided the following:

> "Passion is the energy that keeps us going, that keeps us filled with meaning, and happiness, and anticipation."
> "Passion is a powerful force in accomplishing anything you set your mind to, and in experiencing work and life [to] the fullest extent possible."
> "Ultimately, passion is the driving force behind success and happiness that allows us all to live better lives."

Additionally, in my opinion, passion could also be an unquenchable desire, motivated by a life-altering experience. Are some passions fueled by a positive or negative experience? Most often, yes. Many organizations have been formed because of one person's passion to erase an injustice; i.e., Mothers Against Drunk Drivers (M.A.D.D.). A person's passion will often regulate their attitude. Their positive attitude and values will put a safeguard on their passion and give a minds-eye view on how to direct their energy and determination.

Once you can identify your passion, or what you are passionate about, you should realize the connection to energy and how to preserve it, which will be talked about in a later chapter. The exploration of meaning, the pursuit of happiness, and thrill of lingering anticipation are romantically linked to passion.

Certain things keep you up at night. But the things that you don't mind keeping you up are tied to what you are passionate about. No one has to push you to do the thing that you are most passionate about. You want to do it. It at times seems all-consuming. You get it. It gets you. The mood appears always right once you can pull away and engage the thing which captures your thoughts and attention.

A person with true passion has hope in the midst of life's difficulties. Take Nelson Mandela who spend more than twenty years in imprisonment in South Africa. Where some would have given up the burning desire to brush up against apartheid, he did not. He spent many nights in those undesirable quarters. His passion lived on despite the unrelenting conditions he faced daily.

Mandela said, "There is no passion to be found playing small—in settling for a life that is less than the one you are capable of living."

Ask yourself: 'why am I here?' Or, 'what is my purpose for living?' Or perhaps this question, 'is there a reason I am here and still have hope?'

Barbara Corcoran, a successful business woman and also known from the hit television program Shark Tank, stated that "You can't fake passion."

Passion is something real, emerging from within, expansions of ideas somehow either innately embedded from early childhood or an infusion of how we responded to things in life, our environment. An example of this is when my first grade teacher asked me what I wanted to be when I grew up. While standing near the classroom door that day, I responded by saying that I wanted to be a doctor. My only recollection of a doctor was the late Dr. Max Johnson, our family physician. There was something about him that captured my attention and the respect of others. Although I didn't become a physician, I realized the need to teach, to help people who were in uncertain places, looking for answers to life's deepest questions.

Apple's founder, Steve Jobs, at some point expressed, "You have to be burning with an idea, or a problem, or a wrong that you want to right. If you're not passionate enough from the start, you'll never stick it out."

You have probably heard the story of Michael Jordan, famed ex-basketball player turned billionaire, who was allegedly cut from his high school basketball team. Some accounts say it never happened. Whatever the case, Michael had to work hard to fulfill the passion that was within him. In a later chapter, we will talk about the role of determination in winning and success.

Passion Alone Is Not Enough

Passion alone is not enough, especially if you want to lead   others. That would be like thinking that desire without direction and a vehicle could get you to your destination. Bill George (Northouse, 2013, pp. 258-259) provides his "Authentic Leadership Approach" that includes passion with purpose. He asserts, authentic leaders demonstrate five basic characteristics:

1. They understand their purpose.
2. Have strong values about the right thing to do.
3. Establish trusting relationships with others.
4. Demonstrate self-discipline and act on their values.
5. They are passionate about their mission.

George connects a number of key relationships between passion and purpose, behavior and values, connectedness and relationships, consistency and self-discipline, and compassion and heart.

As I work with leaders in organizations, I continually find it important to ascertain what awareness the leadership has to their own purpose. Often what comes to mind is the emotional intelligence popularized by Daniel Goleman and the need for each leader to have self-awareness as a starting point.

Zenger and Folkman (2009) believe that passion must intersect with organizational needs, and that the "outcome is always positive for the individual and for the organization" (p.116). They further suggest that one key intersection should center on competence. Passion shifts over time for some people.

To better understand your passions, according to Dalton and Thompson (cited in Zenger and Folkman, p.114), it would be helpful to ask yourself the following questions:

- "What do I really enjoy doing?

- What events bring me a great deal of personal satisfaction?
- Which activities energize me in such a way that they hold my interest? When do I lose all sense of time?
- What activities do I daydream about or imagine myself doing?"

There are times when you may not know what to ask, so these and other questions add framework to the whole conceptualization surrounding passion.

The work of Jim Collins (2001), in his book Good to Great, further amplifies the role of passion in his Hedgehog Concept. He provides his readers with three circles that intercept: What You Are Deeply Passionate About, What You Can Be Best in The World At, and What Drives Your Economic Engine. According to Collins, all three circles are needed.

My thinking reflects upon the work of my uncles, Mervin and Dr. Melvin Steals, when I was just a teenager. They seemed to always work day and night on their music. Their pin names became Maestro and Lyric. Since those days they have recorded more than 100 songs, several of which became hits, like the one recorded by the Spinners (Could It Be I'm Falling in Love?).

Even though they were not aware of Jim Collins, they somehow, like many others, embrace the embodiment of the Hedgehog Concept which included "core values and purpose" (Collins, p. 203). Collins' BHAG (Big Hairy Audacious Goals) which ought to propel every passionate person to think big, dream big, and plan big.

Zenger, Folkman, Sherman and Steel (2012) suggest that passion alone is not enough. Their CPO Model includes passion, but they believe that in order to effectively charge your batteries, you have to add competence and organizational need. This age of technology has expanded our reach beyond the walls of the local organization to a more global audience. Because of this, global competitiveness is driving leaders in the workplace to seek out highly-skilled, cutting-edge people. Where passion matters much, competence or mastery (Senge, 2006) are also key elements.

Things Can Derail Your Passion

There appears to be an unseen enemy or force that randomly and strategically places obstacles in the path of a passionate person. In the medieval days, it wasn't uncommon to pave the road to your castle with stones or large rocks to tire the enemy's feet, making them tired and more difficult for them to fight; or even now to lay the enemy's path with landmines to slow their attack or kill their plan or dream of winning. For me, the rocks that were thrown in my path were stepping stones that forced me down a road with a higher calling for myself and others.

When I think of obstacles on the road of passion, I can think of many which will be discussed in the next chapter on attitude. But at this juncture I thought it importance to reference the work of Lencioni (2002) where dysfunction sets in. It is possible to have dysfunction by one or more members of the team. If you are experiencing dysfunction of any type, the full force of passion cannot move forward of upward.

Of Lencioni's five dysfunctions, which include absence of trust, fear of conflict, lack of commitment, avoidance of accountability, and inattention to results, you must always be self-aware of what feeds or starves your passion. You must become the gatekeeper or the driver behind the wheel. I would urge you to keep a close eye on the potential negative impact status and ego, low standards, ambiguity, artificial harmony, and invulnerability that may also be on your road to winning and success (p.174).

Unknowingly, at about eight years old, my road was being paved by a third-grade teacher who caused me to emotionally drop out of school. I had been the student she called upon to help struggling students in her classroom. But on this one day, I decided to share my choral experience with my twin who was not a part of the choral class. I allowed him to take my place, the teacher found out, and I was abruptly removed permanently from any future choral classes. Because I didn't understand why I was being punished for that action, I lost my passion for school emotionally and (I believe) became no longer passionate for school.

By the time I arrived in high school, a counselor told my mom that my twin and I were not college material, but mom was adamant about our potential and said, "my boys are going to college." Mom was an educator and her belief reignited our passion. Years later, my twin brother, Michael, and I received our master's degree during the same ceremony in which our mom received her Ph.D. A few years later, I received my Ph.D. by the age of thirty while working two jobs, experiencing the birth of our two children, and the strict time limits and rigor of the dissertation process. The night I brought my wife home from the hospital after delivering our second child, in an attempt to meet the dissertation deadline, I wrote 90 typed pages in 48 hours (pre-computer days).

The things that can derail your passion can also become a catalyst that can fuel your passion and attitude forward.

Knowing What Fuels Passionate People

Life and work present their own types of disruptions and potential derailments to being passionate. I have seen leaders start the day on a high note and end the day on the lowest possible emotions. You know this happens way too often, but there are ways to prepare, knowing that "passionate people, overall, do live happier and better lives than the average individual" (Hudson, 2014).

When you look at what passionate people do, you are really looking for common habits suggested by author Henri Junttila in an online piece titled The 20 Essential Habits of Highly Passionate People (http://www.wakeupcloud.com/passionate-habits/). A listing of them of this goes this way:

Essential Habits

1.	Excitement	11.	Acceptance
2.	Courage	12.	Generous
3.	Determination	13.	Non-Balance
4.	Positivity	14.	Personal Power
5.	Single-Mindedness	15.	Happiness
6.	Growth-Oriented	16.	Fun
7.	Selective	17.	Perspective
8.	Non-Perfectionistic	18.	Realistically
9.	Prioritized	19.	Conditionally Open-Minded
10.	Self-Motivated	20.	Excuse-Free

It's easy to understand that not all of these habits seem to surface at the same but rather represent something that has developed from within over a period of time.

Certain things intrude on personal behavior, including things in your environment, the things that we experience, places we have been, a composite of hopes and dreams, even passionate people may exhibit a number of these habits over time.

Management of one's day and affairs set the groundwork for such a passionate life. In part, it's self-recognition that is another part of the components of emotional intelligence (Goleman, 2006).

Passion About Work Brings Success

The look of love is not limited to how two people display it and onlookers observe it. There is something about their eyes. There is something about the way they move. There is something about the way they touch or handle their surroundings.

When you relate passion to work, it is often very clear who loves what they do. Article contributor Amy Rees Anderson on Forbes.com (2013) suggests that passion usually has nothing to do with money. That isn't to say that passionate people ought not get paid or should not be rewarded for their work contributions, but that money is probably not their key motivating factor. Whether that passion is tied to a specific industry, like education, ministry, law, or science, desire is what really rings deep within them. Some people just want to help others or find answers to life's most probing questions.

Amy Rees Anderson states, "once you identify your passion you can really begin to figure out what roads lie ahead that will allow you to pursue it (Forbes.com, February 27, 2013). She further talks about how Warren Buffett, "in giving secrets to success," expressed the importance of finding what brings meaning to your life and making it the focus each day. Many of us think often about people and purpose, and what it means to live out such purpose to the fullest. It is important to consider that that cannot happen without passion.

A long-time colleague and friend, John Stanko wrote a book titled "I Wrote This Book on Purpose...So You Can Know Yours" (1998). In this book, there was a deliberate emphasis on the link between purpose, joy, fulfillment, and finances.

Although you may not immediately see or understand purpose, you can see joy and begin establishing what brings it into your life and the lives of others. Fulfillment is often explored by job satisfaction or personal contentment in life.

The Dots of Passion at Work

There are some who believe that you can create a motivating work climate, and if so, then the question would be how. Other questions toward leadership and what they must do through leadership inspire and maximize work passion and performance. The Ken Blanchard Companies (2011) conducted research from which eight key factors emerged:

```
Factors That Drive Work Passion

    Meaningful Work

    Autonomy

    Collaboration

    Fairness

    Recognition

    Growth

    Connectedness to Colleagues

    Connectedness to Leader
```

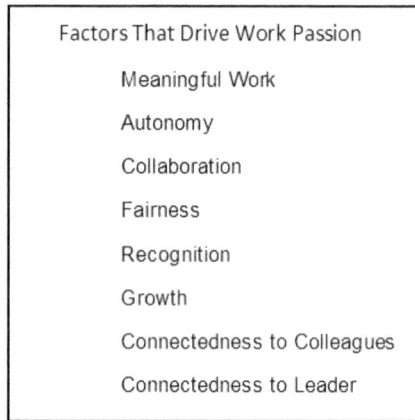

They report a review of literature that produced up to 33 possible factors, which used with factor analysis, ultimately include six of the original factors identified by the Blanchard Companies (Growth, Connectedness to Leader, Meaningful Work, Autonomy, Fairness, and Collaboration). Collectively, an array of factors is dependent upon each other to spark and keep alive that special something from within that we call passion.

In an article titled "Five Ways to Improve Employee Engagement Now," Robyn Reilly through Gallup (2014), said that "Engaged employees are rare." She cites Gallup's State of the Global Workplace report where only 13% of worldwide employees is rare. New Zealand has the highest engaged employees at 23%, Australia at 24%, with the United States only having 30% workplace engagement. This information has only changed by one percentage point (then 29% engagement) in Tucker's 2002 Gallup article.

Agreeing that no one factor alone influences work passion, the Blanchard Companies (2011, p. 9) states, "Employee Work Passion is an individual's persistent, emotionally positive, meaning-based state of well-being stemming from reoccurring cognitive and affective appraisals of various job and organizational situations, which results in consistent, constructive work intentions and behaviors."

Getting Your Passion Back

If you can connect on what passion is and may have lost it at some point, you may wonder how to get it back. An awareness must exist of who you are and what motivates you may shed light through emotional intelligence on what sparks you. Accepting that passion as an emotion helps, and can be turned on, turned up, turned off, given the inward self-reflection and recognition. Your restart button can be pushed internally or externally. Getting charged or becoming passionate again is every part of recognizing what matters most and what to do about it.

Asking yourself a few questions could help in the discovery of the need to get your passion back:

1. What gets you started each day?
2. What are some of the things that propel you into daily tasks?
3. What makes you willing to start early and stay late on projects?
4. What would you do even if no one paid you to do it?
5. Why do you keep working on projects when everyone else is quitting?
6. What do you really love doing often?

If you can you use these questions as prompts for the need to restart passion, you may be able to help others find their passion or get moving again toward self-fulfillment and self-satisfaction.

Kenneth A. Tucker (2002), in a gallup.com business journal, quotes Inspirational Leadership writer Lance Secretan who said that "Few people discover the work they love...." This wouldn't be true about Herb Kelleher, founder and chairman of Southwest Airlines, who had a way of exciting his employees and expecting the same type of passion toward work from new hires.

The passion bar needs to be raised high in an organization. Tucker (2002) says, "Passion helps to engage an organization."

It should be no secret to leaders interested in a passionate work environment to garner the factors that matter most to employees. What we communicate and how we communicate seem to be important hinges that keep the door open for inspiring others. Every manager and leader should not only know themselves well, but should know their people and see where the passion flows.

Not much has changed over the years in some work environments. When considering great workplaces, Tucker (2002) suggested the following:

- Identify the strengths of all employees
- Hire people for the right jobs
- Hire great managers who are engaged and passionate (to help others)
- Create an environment that encourages more engagement and passion
- Give employees opportunity to use their unique strengths
- Placing employees in roles that stretch their talents and strengths
- Outrageously rewarding employees whose passions drive talents to world-class performance.

This thinking, especially about strengths, lines up with the work of both Marcus Buckingham and Gallup. Anyone wondering their strength as an effective leader should consider this Passion Assessment Tool designed by Wolf (2015, p. 123).

<u>The Highly Effective Leader Passion Assessment Tool</u>

Ask yourself the following questions to determine your level of engagement and passion:

1. Am I energetic and enthusiastic?
2. What do I like about my job?
3. Which areas require me to make an attitude adjustment so I can become more passionate?
4. Can I clearly define my organization's expectations and expectations of myself?
5. Have I created the opportunities required to achieve success (self-initiated passion)?
6. Have I surrounded myself with people who are passionate and committed to achieving organizational goals?
7. Do I believe my work is meaningful?
8. Is what I do important?
9. Even though I'm at the top of the organizational chart, have I taken advantage of training and development opportunities that allow me to increase my level of passion?
10. Do I tap into my talents each day, or am I simply coasting?
11. Do I embrace innovation and new ideas, or do I tend to be complacent?
12. Am I emotionally committed to my job?
13. Do I have a good social network?
14. Do I lead by modeling high performance?
15. Do I allow fear to compromise my job satisfaction?

A Nickols Worth Keys

Passion can be viewed in a number of ways by numerous people, but my thought is that passion is like a throttle. It's a forward-moving motion that propels and person from within. That propulsion may not be enough, but never too much. If passion were a mode of transportation, I would put it as one of the must-haves in order to own it. Forget the sputtering and stalling which some vehicles experience. Passion keeps the vehicle in drive when you need propulsion for the next plateau.

With that said, here are my five key points to ponder before we consider the role of attitude on our road to winning and success:

1. The absence of personal passion leads to a life without flavor.
2. The absence of professional passion makes organizational inputs bland.
3. Passionate people in the workplace are like a refreshing stream.
4. They lift loads on heavy emotional days.
5. They are the sunshine on cloudy days.

Passionate people provide answers when others question their adequate significance to workplace productivity. They somehow mine for buried treasures of purpose and add meaning to one's current existence. It should be no surprise that every leader loves a passionate person because when others deviate from the tasks at hand, the passionate person knows how to redirect effort in order to fully search out destiny.

If there is a recall when passion existed, it's necessary to get that passion back.

Chapter 2
Attitude

The greater part of our happiness or misery depends upon our dispositions, and not upon our circumstances.

—Martha Washington

S omewhere in time, Martha Washington figured out the mental angle one must take to have the right attitude or outlook in life. Our response to life's offerings, things that we face on a day-to-day basis, too often dictate how we handle things so often out of our personal control. Realizing that attitude makes a difference prompts us to not only safeguard the right attitude, but to also know how to maintain that attitude and remain passionate about our outlook on both life and in the workplace.

Zenger and Folkman (2009) assert that there is a relationship between attitudes, character and behavior. So often in today's society, the question of character comes up. When it does, a light often shines on one's behavior. Personal behavior should always be monitored. We should be able to take a step back and see if we are carrying ourselves in an acceptable manner. Instead of wondering how we look to others, we should first wonder how we look to ourselves. What's our behavior? How do we really look? What is my appearance from head to toe? Are the things that I say acceptable to me? Will those things said and personal appearance be appropriate to others both inside and outside my personal space?

The authors raise concerns about character also and point toward the link between behavior, attitude, and character sequentially. They say (Zenger and Folkman, 2009, p. 217), "When people learn and practice new behavior, there is a remarkable transformation of their attitudes and ultimately their character."

In some of my work with parents of teens, one of the biggest things that needs addressed frequently is the attitude. I tell the story of having our AA meeting, meaning an attitude adjustment in our own home. If a person's attitude is off, unacceptable, getting anything across becomes labored. This is also true in marriage, as well as in the workplace. My thoughts go back to the work of my doctoral dissertation co-chair, Dr. Kathryn Atman, who about a year prior to embarking on that project, taught a course which involved transactional analysis. The concept was new to me at the time but worth embracing for a lifetime.

As I understood the concept then and reflect upon it now, occasionally people operate between child-adolescent-adult behavior. How many times have we heard that he or she needs to grow up? Or, that they are just acting like a child? In order to grow up, one needs to clearly understand the gravity of making right behavioral choices. Dale Carnegie said, in How to Win Friends and Influence People, "It isn't what you have or who you are or where you are or what you are doing that makes you happy or unhappy. It is what you think about it" (cited in http://www.goodreads.com/quotes/tag/attitude). Sometimes the home can be a very unhappy place. The workplace can also be a very unhappy place. Part of the blame can be placed on our attitude. I wouldn't say that certain things at home don't need changed. I also would suggest that we ignore all the unacceptable workplace behavior coming either from people who are plain old unhappy, complaining about everything behind the back of those in authority. Personal responsibility has to be taken for one's own behavior. Behavior unchecked can lead to character marred beyond imagination.

I recall the story of a lady who worked in a nonprofit organization that helped a lot of people. During the first few years of employment, everything seemed to be going well. Complaints were at a minimum, then something began to happen. She began complaining more and more. It wasn't that she didn't enjoy helping people anymore, it was just that her boss for whatever reason had begun to change. His attitude had shifted about how he did his job and how he talked negatively to her and perhaps others in the workplace. Hearing enough of her complaining, one day I suggested that she take a look at the "Serenity Prayer."

Now I haven't had a personal experience with drugs and alcohol, but I was very much aware of that prayer and its focus on not only God but also on the courage needed to accept the things we cannot change. My message to her was really simple, change your attitude about how you see what's going on. Making attitude adjustments can be rather difficult. But it is well within our power to do so.

The work of McKnight and Chapman (2010, p. 9) states that "Attitude is your general disposition—your mental 'starting place' for viewing life and the people and events in it." Both of them agree that you can adjust your mental image of any situation to reflect the positive side of things. Where some spend a lot of time of situations they cannot change, it becomes crucial to explore possibilities. When the necessary change to move forward appears to be painful, it seems easier to stay stuck where you are and suffer than to move on to what is perceived to be worse and suffer. Too many people get stuck and overly mired when it may be the time to move on to what might work versus no movement at all.

Positive Attitude Makes a Difference

Think about the people you know who are just unable to move forward. They may feel that they have a legitimate reason for their feelings and disposition. But the lack of progress must be noted. In some of my work with people who have been emotionally wounded, I have heard people using what was done or said to them as justifiable barriers to their bad attitude. In some cases, people have become victimized by toxic behavior in the workplace.

It is not hard to concur with the views of McKnight et al. (2010, p.14) when they highlight the following benefits of people who have chosen to look forward and upward:

➢ See more opportunities and are more likely to spot problems in time to avoid major consequences.
➢ Are more likely to work to higher standards of quality, safety, and productivity.
➢ Are always looking out for other people, and this teamwork improves overall quality, safety, and productivity.
➢ Are more desirable to work with—and the work is more enjoyable.
➢ Are more likely to be promoted to more responsible jobs; they are more likely to move up and forward.

Fritz (2008) expands on the idea of building a positive attitude by stating, "Building a positive attitude begins with having confidence in yourself. Confidence reinforces ability, doubles energy, buttresses mental faculties, and increases power."

Too often we are not cognizant of the impact or level of positive influence we can have on others around us. The interesting thing is that both our verbal and nonverbal communication comes into play. In a recent consultation with a few administrators, the deep concern was about changing the workplace culture. They had fallen victim to scrutiny as an organization because of the behavior of a few people. The organization's reputation has become damaged due to media exposure. My thinking in part was based upon the work of an MIT professor named Edgar Schein (2009), who wrote about the three elements of culture.

Schein suggested that those three elements of culture involved artifacts, espoused values, and underlying basic assumptions. Artifacts would reflect those surface things that can be seen or heard in the workplace. Because of what this organization and so many like them are facing around the U.S., for example school districts, police departments, and corporations, something visible needs to be exhibited to represent changes in attitude about certain negative behaviors.

It was Winston Churchill who once said, "Attitude is a little thing that makes a big difference." From a leadership perspective, we should model the attitude that we want saturating our work environment.

Clearly understanding how needful and intentional we must be about fostering the right attitude helps us consider the benefits associated. Fritz (2008, p. 111) says, effective leaders convey attitude importance and move the organization forward basically by:

- Making things mutually beneficial
- Helping people be successful
- Earning respect
- Avoiding humiliating assignments or directives
- Favoring those who get the best results
- Not expecting to be popular—look for respect

- Delivering on commitments, without overpromising, yet getting participation in goal-setting.

Any person or leaders with a positive attitude are often being watched by those as peers or subordinates today. It matters not if they complement or confront you about your behavior, take seriously that they are taking notes regularly.

Successful Leaders Have Key Characteristics

Displaying a positive attitude over a period of time would typically have the reward of influence upon others in the workplace. Fritz (2008, pp. 29-30) reports that successful leaders:

- ❖ Have high frustration tolerance.
- ❖ Encourage participation.
- ❖ Continually question themselves.
- ❖ Control impulses to get even.
- ❖ Win without exulting.
- ❖ Lose without moping.
- ❖ Recognize legal, ethical, and moral restrictions.
- ❖ Are conscious of group loyalties.
- ❖ Have realistic goals.

He goes on to say, "A positive attitude also ignites the drive to excel in yourself and those around you" (p. 30).

Those claims appear to be supported through the work of both Alexander Hill (1997), Warren Bennis (1994), and Craig E. Johnson (2001) in their books Just Business, On Becoming A Leader, and Meeting the Ethical Challenges of Leadership, respectively. Too often the real staple for engaging others in a positive manner is connected to the positive attitude of the leader. It somehow also gives greater reason why good and successful leaders attempt to safeguard their positive attitude. The impact provides a basis for good leadership to adequately bring resolve in the workplace by 1) solving personal conflicts quickly, 2) taking the high road when people when others behave unreasonably or unfairly, and 3) being able to insulate or distance yourself when reporting conflicts with someone (McKnight et al., 2010).

Creating and Maintaining a Positive Attitude

The challenge of maintaining a positive attitude in this fluid, ever-changing world could prove to be a daunting, almost insurmountable task. In my work with executives, managers, and boards, the thought of suggesting an iron-clad approach that never changes would weaken one's credibility. So allow me to provide some tips to consider, based upon the suggestions of Craig Dewe, and Marelisa Fabrega, each as online contributors.

In his piece on maintaining a positive attitude, Dewe (2016) provides 11 tips:

1. You Determine Your Reality
2. Start Your Day Strong
3. Exercise Is The Natural Feel Good Good
4. Use Books, Audio and Videos to Overload Your Brain with Positivity
5. Your Language Shapes Your Thoughts
6. Hang Out With Positive People
7. Show Your Appreciation For Others
8. Garbage In, Garbage Out
9. Stop Negative Thoughts In Their Tracks
10. Live With Gratitude
11. Recharge Your Batteries.

When Marelisa Fabrega (2016) shares her 21 Ways to Create and Maintain a Positive Attitude, the following list shows some likenesses:

1.	Have a Morning Routine
2.	Carry An Attitude of Happiness With You
3.	Relish Small Pleasures
4.	Smile
5.	Upload Positivity to Your Brain
6.	Take Responsibility
7.	Have a Zen Attitude
8.	Be Proactive
9.	Change Your Thoughts
10.	Have a Purpose
11.	Focus On the Good
12.	Stop Expecting Life to Be Easy
13.	Keep Up Your Enthusiasm
14.	Give Up On Having An Attitude of Entitlement
15.	Visualize
16.	Limit Your Complaints
17.	Watch Your Words
18.	Use The Power of Humor
19.	Use Gratitude to Improve Your Attitude
20.	Develop an Attitude of Curiosity
21.	Seek Out Others With a Positive Attitude

Some of the work of Oakley and Krug (1991) with emphasis upon creative and reactive thinking further authenticates the basis of Dewe and Fabrega's tips. The worth of transporting these tips into one's daily routines makes you 1) happier, 2) more resilient, 3) improves your relationships, 4) increases your chances of success in any endeavor, 5) makes you more creative, and 6) helps you make better decisions (Fabrega, 2016).

Our response to others and to situations in the workplace speaks volumes about our own attitudinal grounding. Just take a look at the amount of validation, competition, creativity, and retention that subsists around you. Ask yourself if there are any ties to negative or positive attitude (Root, 2016).

A Nickols Worth Keys

If you used what I call an attitudinal atmospheric gauge, you might be able to gain insight into how high you can go to help you survey the conditions in the air. There are times no words are expressed but you can sense what's going on. Absent of specificity, something either gives you a good feeling or the idea that something is not right. Attitudes or moods can be rather pervasive. Every leaders needs to know how to maneuver through what could either be a toxic workplace or the makings of a very promising work environment. So, keep these things in mind:

1. Good attitudes make things good for all, not just some.
2. Bad attitudes are like people driving into other people's lanes, or taking their half of the road out of the middle.
3. Where we cannot control every situation or circumstance, we can maintain a constant, even kiln in our approaches.
4. The lack of reliance on fuses increases our need for a breaker system. Good attitude sparks good responses from others.
5. A person on top of their own attitude ought to be able to arouse the expectations of others.

Also, be aware that your attitude or the attitude of your sphere of influence can paralyze you in your tracks or catapult you further down the road to winning and success.

Every person who has grown to a degree of usefulness, every person who has grown to distinction, almost without exception has been a person who has risen by overcoming obstacles, by removing difficulties, by resolving that when he met discouragement he would not give up.

—Booker T. Washington

Chapter 3
Values

Enlightened leadership is spiritual if we understand spirituality not as some kind of religious dogma or ideology but as the domain of awareness where we experience values like truth, goodness, beauty, love and compassion, and also intuition, creativity, insight and focused attention.

—Deepok Chopra

This quote by Deepok Chopra provides hints to both the enlightened leader and awareness of various values. It was Oakley and Krug (1991) who earlier expounded on how an enlightened leader is characterized. A clearly defined understanding of values, both personally and organizationally, must be understood first for any leader. How those values are espoused, some of which become core values, can later yield the desired behaviors in the workplace culture.

29

The work of Edgar Schein (2009), an MIT professor, brought us much meaning to survival in the corporate culture. That work in part entailed the three elements of culture: Artifacts, Espoused Values, and Shared Tacit Assumptions. He said, "The first things you learn when you start asking questions is that the organization has certain values that are supposed to create an image of the organization" (p. 23). But he in this context was the organization which is made up of more than one individual.

Pinder (1998) didn't concede that values are behaviors. He stated, "values are neither attitudes nor behaviors. Instead, values are the very building blocks of the behavior of and choices made by individuals" (p. 69). He goes on to say that those same values make up the "essence" of the culture (p. 73). Kilmann (1981) expands our understanding of values by suggesting that "values can be guides to what needs, wants, desires people should have, what interests, preferences, and goals are seen as desirable or undesirable, what individual dispositions or traits one ought to have, and what beliefs and attitudes individuals should express" (p. 942).

Values are seen as those things which come after needs but before attitudes and behaviors, sequentially (Kilmann, 1981). He figured in would look something like this:

Needs---------Values-----------Attitudes--------Behaviors
    Needs---------Values-----------Attitudes--------Behaviors

Kilmann also believes values serve as the "basis for making choices" (p. 69). Bad values are linked to bad choices. Good values are on the other hand linked to good choices. Organizations don't make choices, people do. An increase in understanding exists when we consider that "values are objects, qualities, standards, or conditions that satisfy or are perceived to satisfy needs and/or that act as guides to human action" (p. 68).

Ismail (2016, p. 30) maintains as others that values have some influence on human choices. In his work, he makes reference to the work of a number of researchers to support his assertion. He reports the following work of George W. England:

1. Personal value systems influence a manager's perception of the situations and problems he faces.
2. Personal value systems influence a manager's decisions and solutions to problems.
3. Personal value systems influence the way in which a manager looks at other individuals and groups of individuals; thus, they influence interpersonal relationships.
4. Personal value systems influence the perception of individual and organizational success as well as their achievement.
5. Personal value systems set the limits for the determination of what is and what is not determined as ethical behavior by a manager.
6. Personal value systems influence the extent to which a manager will accept or resist organizational pressures and goals.

Every leader should want to identify their values and search out how those values may be impacting their organization.

What Are Your Values?

The editorial team of MindTools (Editorial Team, 2016) insists that the undermentioned things are true about values:

• Your values are the things that you believe are important in the way you live and work.
• They (should) determine your priorities, and, deep down, they're probably the measures you use to tell if your life is turning out the way you want it to.
• When the things you do and the way you behave match your values, life is usually good—you're

satisfied and content. But when these don't align with your personal values, that's when things feel...wrong.

The Editorial Team further agrees, "Values exist, whether you recognize them or not." So, as a leader, you must make every effort or plan to honor those values. Never give the appearance by honoring bad, undesirable values. It is always good to have honorable values, the ones that honor your people, those within your sphere of impact; those who rely on you to do the right things all the time.

The tie to happiness leaves us a clear-cut clue as to whether we are on the right road. As a leader, or in any capacity, ask yourself if you are bringing happiness to the people around you (Gottschalk, 2013). Do they appear to be happy with you? Is there an apparent amount of satisfaction or fulfillment with the work or investment of personal commitment toward them or what's important to their future success?

A sampling of values from the MindTools Editorial Team is listed here:

Accountability	Discipline	Fairness
Assertiveness	Enthusiasm	Happiness
Commitment	Excellence	Honesty
Justice	Sensitivity	Teamwork
Loyalty	Mastery	Strategic
Openness	Service	Vision
Growth	Altruism	Community

When an organization, for example, values accountability, the leadership becomes clear on expectations and transparency. Measures are put into place through policies and procedures to not only hold some people accountable, but to make accountability the expectation for everyone. Top leadership find ways to make themselves also accountable and true to the mission of the organization. The same can be said about mastery or teamwork or commitment.

In this highly competitive, global marketplace, values address needs and shape attitudes once embraced. The commitment to mastery requires teamwork. This is evidenced in Peter Senge's Fifth Discipline which puts forth the art and practices of a learning organization. The learning organization encompasses what Senge (2006) discusses in detail:

1. Personal mastery where you regularly clarify and deepen personal vision, focus on energies, develop patience, and see reality with objectivity.
2. Mental models that have deeply ingrained assumptions, images, and generalizations which influence our understanding of the world and the actions we take.
3. Building shared visions which include shared pictures of our future that promote commitment willingly without coercion.
4. Team learning with frequent conversations and openness that includes participation by all concerned as stakeholders.
5. Systems thinking which is a thorough integration of the four previous disciplines.

A recall of the Schein (2009) elements of culture confirms they are embedded in the work Senge and undoubtedly many others.

Questions Help with Operating Values and Behaviors

Leaders should always show a willingness to step back and look at what is working or not working in the cultures. Questions become a key way to get at what's happening and prudent leaders allow what Oakley and Krug (1991) refer to as the framing of effective questions (EQ's). Arguably, Cloud (2013, p. 191) provides a list of questions for fruitful discussion among the entire leadership team regarding operating values and behaviors:

- What is the team's collective purpose?
- What do you want this team to accomplish?
- If that is what you want to accomplish, then what does this team need to look at in order to pull that off?
- How does it need to operate?
- What values will bring that vision to reality?
- How do those values relate specifically to the vision, goals, etc.?
- How will they drive them?
- What behaviors will demonstrate and drive those values?
- How do we need to behave to make sure it all happens?

The Link Between Purpose and Improved Leadership

No matter how we might want to drift away for the importance of values, it's just not that simple. It was in the chapter on passion that we also mentioned purpose. They are inextricably connected. The same might be said of the relationship between purpose, values, and improving leadership.

In a Huffington Post blog, Anne Loehr (2014) reiterates the key role values play on the things that matter most, what you stand for, and how "it creates and maintains company culture, informs employee selection, guides the direction of company growth, and adds meaning to the work required to maintain the organization." Too often these things are not a part of our thinking about values, but should be considered in our pursuit to see the organization through the lens of those in leadership positions.

It would be uncommon to initially sense the link between purpose and leadership, but a skilled listener and cognitively perceptive leadership ability heightens the growth of that leader. The use of personal core values comes into play, especially where most "people have approximately 5-7 core values that identify who they are at the core," according to Loehr. It takes a sensitivity to what we do on a daily basis at both home and work. She also thinks that the leader's strong values support the organizational culture. The flip side of this thinking could lead us to believe that negative behavior rooted in differentiated values can have adverse consequences in the workplace. When leaders take the strong values approach towards their followers, Northouse (2013, p.259) believes, "They have a clear idea of who they are, where they are going, and what the right thing is to do."

Personal Value System and Work-Life Balance

Where open discussion is not common regarding a leader's personal life, while in a work setting, some attention needs to be given to such a critical area. We have been hearing about work-life balance for quite some time, but the thought of connecting it to our personal value system may have some merit.

Watching people from a variety of professions, or in search of that one thing that they think brings out their passion, I have seen a number of people get lost in the things being pursued. As important as work is, and the growing demand on our time and energy, we should not ignore the relationship to values, especially personal values.

Hereford (essentiallifeskills.net) agrees with others who have conceded that values help define your character, but goes further to say that one has to view values in four categories: personal, spiritual, family, and career. Personal values are said to include the things you see worth aspiring to and bring definition to character. Spiritual values help us in connecting to a higher power and take us beyond any purpose tied to material existence. Family values are seen in the care of those to whom we are close, including our spouse, children, friends, parents, or other family members. One's career values involve the best use of our talents and skills with overall contribution to societal issues or compensatory rewards. Yet the author doesn't leave out some of the special values such as integrity, respect, loyalty, and responsibility.

For years, the growing conversations in the workplace have centered on work-life balance. The very soul of a person is somehow helped or harmed by not only how we treat people in the workplace but also by those who look to and rely upon us to do the right things concerning their well-being. There are some things we shouldn't want to get wrong with respect to removing risk and accelerating success (Daum, 2016). Northouse (2013, p. 259) takes the position that "Authentic leaders understand their own values and behave toward others based on these values." In some cases, that could be a very good thing, but in others not so good if the leader in the home or the work culture doesn't have a clue. Northouse asserts further that they will compromise their values and gain strength in their values situationally.

Groysberg and Abrahams (2014) through a Harvard Business Review article wrote additionally about the possibility of both managing your work and your life. They discovered "that prospering in the senior ranks is a matter of carefully combining work and home so as to lose themselves, their loved ones, or their foothold on success." They drew on data from five years of interviews of approximately 4,000 executives worldwide with the help of Harvard Business School students and 82 executives surveyed in Harvard's leadership course. There were revelations as to how they attempted to manage multi-tasking and the use of a good support network, while balancing the real needs their families faced like any other family. The bottom line is that not only is it worth balancing work and life, but that it is essential to value it highly through prioritization.

A Nickols Worth Keys

What leaders do is of such utmost importance. What they believe, how they carry themselves, what they value may have direct consequence or uplifting benefits in the lives of everyone in their presence on a regular and ongoing basis. It should become incumbent upon anyone in a leadership capacity to:

1. Identify your true values carefully.
2. Develop a personal values system that reflects your true self.
3. Give strong reflection on the impact those personal values have on your life choices and those of others around you.
4. Always keep in your view the times when you were not true to those values, especially when things turned into a mess.
5. Make sure those values help in work-life balance and are examined daily as core to what matters most.

If you are willing to do more than you are paid to do, eventually you will be paid to do more than you do.

—Anonymous

Chapter 4
Energy

Your energy is one of your biggest assets and must be managed.
—Dr. Henry Cloud

One of the things that may be worse than a depleted checking account is a deleted personal energy reserve. Another example that many people can relate to is trying to drive a distance long after the gas gauge indicated that there is a need for fuel. The second example reminds me of a trip from a resort in the western mountains of Massachusetts to a family visit in Ayer, Massachusetts. In addition to having to recalculate the distance and time required there and back, I needed to determine the amount fuel required. Well, I got the distance right but did not anticipate that the remaining fuel would not be enough to get us back to the resort.

When this miscue in fuel level occurs in the workplace, days are longer and resources, especially human resources, are stretched. With all the questions that can surround ascertaining our passion, adjusting our attitude, and vetting our values, energy review and conservation becomes equally essential on the road to winning and success. If you're in a boat without a motor or a paddle, you may slowly drift along or become stymied. Like, being without energy, you would lack the momentum needed to propel you down the straight and narrow road, and out of the way of traps, speed bumps, ruts or detours. The road more desired entails the self-injection of energy versus total reliance upon someone else and won't convey the realities we often face. Everyone must take some responsibility. To that end, Cloud (2013, p. 151) says, "Injecting people with energy and a new sense of power and control is a huge part of what leadership is about."

Energy Is Everything//Creating A Personal Energy Management Profile (2015) suggested that everyone has a personal energy profile. Not paying attention to that profile means that energy level and causation could be all over the place. In other words, we need to track the highs and lows of energy expenditure and the related reasons why. It's not hard to concede that we all probably gain energy from the things we love most. Chances are, due to our passion and adjusted attitudes, even with daunting and demanding tasks, we just do them if we are passionate about the tasks at hand and value a high level of importance to complete them successfully.

Managing Energy, Not Time

Managing time has its own set of challenges. There are only so many hours in the day. Just in case you haven't noted, we still have only 24 hours and then off to the next day. Because of work demands or the need to meet expectations in the workplace, many people work well into the early morning of the next day to reach deadlines, while others are expected to communicate with a global team member. The old 8-hour work day rarely exists for people of passion or where the boss says, "This has to be done by tomorrow."

Busy moms and dads, managing daily household chores, engaging in a child's life from birth through at least high school, requires a unique set of skills or techniques to keep all the balls they juggle in the air. Chapman and Rupured (2016) provide the following sample of strategies for time management:

> ➢ Know How You Spend Your Time
> ➢ Set Priorities
> ➢ Use a Planning Tool
> ➢ Get Organized
> ➢ Schedule Your Time Appropriately
> ➢ Delegate: Get Help from Others
> ➢ Stop Procrastinating
> ➢ Manage External Time Wasters
> ➢ Avoid Multi-Tasking
> ➢ Stay Healthy.

They present basic examples of the strategic tips helpful to everyone in every life pursuit. MindTools holds the same belief through articles Banish the Time Bandits! and Minimizing Distractions (2016).

In Minimizing Distractions, the MindTools Editorial Team (2016) takes a perspective that we need to deal with what they consider the 10 most common distractions: 1) Personal Technology, blurred personal and professional use at work; 2) Email, checking it at work frequently; 3) Social Media, excessive use; 4) Instant Messaging, limiting access during work; 5) Browsing, theft of time in the workplace; 6) Phone Calls, disrupting deep concentration; 7) The Work Environment, ; 8) Confusion, unplanned activity; 9) Other People, non-work related visits by other employees; and 10) You, being mentally and physically prepared. Reflected in the Energy Project findings in 2014, "59% of workers are not getting their core needs met at work" (The Energy Project, 2014; Ray, 2016).

Although many organizations have policies that preclude the outside distractions, it requires planning and discipline to stay on task inside the workplace. For example, I recall a problem by a long-term government employee whom I have had the pleasure to mentor over the years. Her call came one morning around 6, and I knew there had to be a problem of some sort. Her growing concern that day was the increasing interruptions from an employee who repeatedly showed up at her desk daily. One of the suggestions I gave her, after asking a series of questions, was that she put that employee on her schedule toward the end of the workday. It seemingly worked because she was able to give that employee the time and attention, but schedule it in such a way to benefit both.

Although there is meaningful application of those strategies outside the workplace, it is also vital to glean the transferability of them in the role of leaders everywhere. Schwartz and McCarthy (2007) share in a Harvard Business Review article how one partner of Ernst & Young, married with four young   children, knew he had a real wrestle on his hands. It was evidenced by his poor sleeping habits, no time to exercise, his failing to eat healthy meals, and eating on the run while working at his desk. This probably sounds like someone you know. Maybe this is even you.

The complexity of the situation was increasingly revealing for the workplace with "declining levels of engagement, increasing levels of distraction, high turnover rates, and soaring medical costs among employees" (Schwartz and McCarthy, 2007). So, at the Energy Project, they began examining the four main wellsprings in human beings: body, emotion, mind, and spirit. This concern caused them to study companies such as Wachovia, Ernst & Young, Sony, Deutsche Bank, Nokia, ING Direct, Ford, and MasterCard. What they found was that employees who participated in an energy program outperformed the control group employees. One outstanding thing was "ultradian rhythms" which exist from high to slower energy exhibition over a 90- to 120-minute cycle.

professional journey that we can handle, stop where appropriate, and recalculate while refreshing or refueling. We need to keep all options open and be willing to readjust certain components to ensure safe completion of the plan.

A Nickols Worth Keys

Instead of saying, burn, burn, burn, we should learn, learn, learn. There are few roads that have not had a traveling of one kind or another. The highest mountains of the world have been scaled again and again. So let's take into account a few things we should embrace on this journey:

1. Plan well and keep in mind both the road to be traveled and how much fuel is required.
2. Never get to the place where you avoid adequate preparation for mind, body, emotions, and spiritually.
3. Plan with others in mind, because what may be taxing to you may also become taxing to everyone on your team.
4. Become a knowledgeable manager of your time and energy.
5. Help those around you become good managers that will keep them in the professional game and avoid burnout.

Chapter 5
Determination

Nothing in this world can take the place of persistence. Talent will not; nothing is more common than unsuccessful men with talent. Genius will not; unrewarded genius is almost a proverb.

—Calvin Coolidge

When we come into this world, we come without guarantees of smooth roads and hopes that we will reach the destinations of choice at specified times. Unpredictable and changing terrain may often surface and at times nothing goes according to plan. You might think that advantages could be gained from all the modern-day technologies that exist. With all the data that exists, certainly we might get advance warning with updates, but that is rarely the case because little is for certain. Determination can be defined as firmness of purpose, resoluteness. You have to be persistent in your determination to finish what has been started, and to finish it in a victorious fashion.

Who you are surfaces when you face ambiguity. Staying the course without panic requires a number of things including self-discipline. Northouse says, "Self-discipline gives leaders focus and determination" (2013, p. 260). The need for motivation is welcomed in unfamiliar surroundings, pointing back to who you are, who you have been, and the motivation to redirect your leadership steps.

Being An Authentic Leader

There are some things you draw upon to help you maneuver through life. You don't become authentic by imitating others. Your life's experiences help you all along the way. This doesn't bar you from the vicarious things you glean from others around you. I can remember the words of the late federal judge, Gary Lancaster, who preceded me in college by several years but had shared in a keynote speech in our area years ago. He said that when he goes to the federal bench, he carries with him all of his life's experiences, everything said to him, everything he had garnered. It somehow shaped his view of the world and what he needed to consider in adjudicating cases in his federal courtroom.

We may not readily admit it, but this is true for us also. The thing that stands out is what we do with those experiences. How we reconfigure both bad and good experiences make us who we are, unique. Something from those vistas in our personal lives aids in making us authentic.

George, Sims, McLean, and Mayer (2007, p. 129) affirm that "We all have the capacity to inspire and empower others. But we must first be willing to devote ourselves to our personal growth and development as leaders." But this journey is said to begin with your own life story and can be put in some context by the following questions (p. 134):

1) Which people and experiences in your early life had the greatest impact on you?
2) What tools do you use to become self-aware?
3) What are your most deeply held values?
4) What motivates you extrinsically?
5) What kind of support team do you have?
6) Is your life integrated?
7) What does being authentic mean in your life?
8) What steps can you take today, tomorrow, and over the next year to develop your authentic leadership?

They also urge anyone wanting to become an authentic leader to practice your values and principles, balance your extrinsic and intrinsic motivations, build your support team, integrate your life by staying grounded, and empower people to lead. Drawing upon the conclusions of a Stanford Graduate School of Business Advisory Council report where 75 members were asked about the most important capacity for the leaders to develop, they found the unanimous response was the need for self-awareness (p.133).

Be Aware of What Successful Leaders Do

Claiming to want success is not enough. That claim must be routed in things discussed in earlier chapters relating passion, attitude, values, energy as part of the composite ingredients toward winning and success. Daum (2013) identifies 8 things that really successful people do. They are briefly listed here:

1. Make Materialism Irrelevant
2. Enhance Knowledge
3. Manage Relationship Expectations
4. Practice Emotional Self-Awareness
5. Commit to a Physical Ideal
6. Gain Clarity About Spirituality
7. Adhere to a Code of Ethics
8. Focus on Time Efficiency.

Tracy (2016) concedes that successful people maintain at least these seven good habits: 1) being goal-oriented, 2) are results driven, 3) are action oriented, 4) are people oriented, 5) are health conscience, 6) are honest, and 7) are self-disciplined. Successful people also have to be determined. Doing this includes the aforementioned tips and an overlap of the suggestions of many others that were previously discussed (Covey, 2013).

Some believe you can learn determination. Perhaps it would be better stated that we can learn from others a few key elements that we should critically embrace. A wikihow.com (2016) link looked at determination and it backed up the thinking that it "is a skill that can be learned!" A portion of that information urges figuring out your type of determination. Pillay (2011) said the types are: uphill determination and coasting determination. Uphill means exactly what it implies, work that depends upon difficulty and obstacles, while coasting determination is about short-term gratification and later reaching for the success of long-term goals. Each type necessitates its own display of will power.

What the Research Says

Size (2016) talks about the view of researchers in determining well-being. They use the science of self-determination, supported by thousands of studies that use self-determination theory as a foundation of their own work. This theory explains motivation, personality and well-being as highly important to have a good life. The theory identifies the need for Autonomy, Competence, and Social Relatedness and must underlie human goals and behaviors.

Two researchers, Deci and Ryan (2008, p. 182; David, 2014; David, 2015) mentioned in the article by Size (2016), state that "self-determination (STD) addresses such basic issues as personality development, self- regulation, universal psychological needs, life goals and aspirations, energy and vitality, nonconscious processes, the relations of culture to motivation, and the impact of social environments on motivation, affect, behavior, and well-being." What they found in their research corroborates information presented in earlier chapters of this book.

The work of Martin Seligman (cited in David, June 2015), called by some as the father of positive psychology, continued the research of many who preceded him. Formerly serving also as the president of the American Psychological Association in 1998, he emphasized three paths to happiness. He highlighted 1) Pleasure, 2) Engagement, and 3) Meaning. Pleasure required focus on maximizing positive emotions. Engagement depended on activities that allowed you to flow with what he called deep and effortless involvement. And the third, meaning, was to serve as the component that goes to what would I call higher, greater real purpose. Seligman later added to the three orientations by linking accomplishment and relationships to his formula PERMA (Pleasure, Engagement, Relationships, Meaning, and Accomplishment).

Facing Hard Times? You're Not Alone

One might think that facing hard times and failure are two sides of the same coin, but they are not. In my life's work, I have encountered people who were given up on and probably would have given up if it were not for their determination. When many people hear the word cancer, they immediately feel that it's their demise, and sudden doom is near. A lady named Cora was diagnosed with cancer more than thirty-five years ago, breast cancer, and she is still around today. Think about the companies that should have folded but held out, reorganized, and they have remained like Chrysler under the then leadership of Lee Iaoccca. Or, what about the late Steve Jobs of Apple? Or, Jack Welsh from G.E. Or, for that matter, the likes of Michael Jordan, ex-NBA basketball player who was said to have struggled making the basketball team? We hear the eventual stories of Jackie Robinson breaking the color barrier in baseball. But what about the struggles of Chuck Cooper who became the first African-American drafted into the NBA by the Boston Celtics?

We have heard about the stories of many others who had the hard roads to travel. You certainly may have your own story, and that story's end is in part to be determined by how you deal with things along the way. Facing and dealing with hard times calls for you not to be mediocre in your status. Those hard times should motivate you to achieve whatever dreams you have. Tej (2012) urges you to question "your why." This is one of the things, while coaching others in organizations and life, that I attempt to get them to use as a focal point. I used to pose that question to people who have either been appointed to a high position or those in pursuit of a higher degree or goal in life. They sometimes struggle when they don't see signs of immediate results. They must remain consistent and determined. Some things become non-negotiables.

Williams (2013) provides 7 non-negotiables that he believes will change your life: Respect, Belief, Trust, Loyalty, Commitment, Courage, and Gratitude. If you can recall, a few of them fit the kinds of values discussed in a previous chapter. Of the seven, commitment stands out here because he says to "Hold nothing back and work like this is your last job." You need to make those obstacles your game-changers!

The Last Bridge May Be Called Fear

You may not have thought about failure as an option, but it may just be your best option. I'm not saying that you dwell on the idea of failing. I am saying that it may be a common thing that happens enough that you need to learn, as Maxwell (2000, p.149) put it, Fail Forward. Because this too requires skill, I thought I would include a parcel of his thinking about failing forward:

Steps to Failing Forward

1. Realize there is one major difference between average people and achieving people.
2. Learn a new definition of failure.
3. Remove the "you" from failure.
4. Take action and reduce your fear.
5. Change your response to failure by accepting responsibility.
6. Don't let the failure from outside get inside you.
7. Say good-bye to yesterday.
8. Change yourself, and your world changes.
9. Get over yourself and start giving yourself.
10. Find the benefit in every bad experience.
11. If at first you do not succeed, try something harder.
12. Learn from a bad experience and make it a good experience.

If you want it, go for it with everything that you have or can find.

A Nickols Worth Keys

A 95-year-old woman with eight children, when they would say to her, "I can't," would say to them, "can't died. With determination, you can be anything and do anything you put your mind to." With only a sixth grade education, she was determined that all eight children would graduate from high school, and they did.

1. Never take "no" for an answer when you find yourself in unfamiliar places.
2. If you start a thing, you probably have enough to finish it well.
3. Every road goes somewhere, so carefully plan your next best trip and enjoy the ride.
4. You have packed inside all the passion, attitude, values, energy, and determination for your current destination.
5. Obstacles and barriers are signs you are on the right road; don't detour you'll reach the finish line.

Conclusions

Things turn out best for the people who make the best of the way things turn out.

—John Wooden

There are times when you feel that some people have a better hand at what they have been dealt in life. The scales of pro versus con, advantages versus disadvantages, short straw versus long straw, allows some people to decide to just flip a coin. The truth may well lie in the way people have responded to life's difficult situations. Everything is not equal. Some people have discovered an unending will to not only live, but the quest to pursue success and win often. Quitting does not become an option.

Attitude has a lot to do with the shaping of behavior. In order to succeed, it is critical to work on your outlook by seriously

55

looking within and setting the course for success. Fritz (2008, p. 105) says that a "positive attitude prompts success."

Fritz (p. 109) suggests that winners recognize the following vital principles in their relationships:

1. Everyone can be motivated in some way.
2. People tend to do things for their reasons.
3. Overextension of a strength can become a weakness.
4. You do not motivate people; you create an environment in which they will be self-motivated.

A lot has to go into how you see yourself, how you see others, and how you choose to prevent obstacles from encouraging a fatalistic point of view.

Winning is not an unusual feat. People have figured out ways to win throughout man's existence. The ability to win is about discovery about your true self and what that will look like once you have achieved it. With purposeful passion, adjustments to attitude, crystalizing personal values that benefit you and those in your sphere, allocating the right amount of energy, and taking an I will not give up approach, you will have demonstrated the conative way of doing things.

While so much focus has been on the affective, behavioral, and cognitive domains, it seems that strength to do and succeed may also rest in the conative domain. Huitt (1999) claims that "Conation refers to the connection of knowledge and affect to behavior and is associated with the issue of 'why.' It is the personal, intentional, planful, deliberate, goal-oriented, or striving component of motivation, the proactive aspect of behavior." He agrees that we face several conative issues daily that raise the following questions:

- What are my intentions and my goals?
- What am I going to do?
- What are my plans and my commitments?

All of these views support my position in the literature shared in this book.

The PAVED Model is my expression of what is needed to win and succeed in both personal pursuits and the actualization of corporate goals:

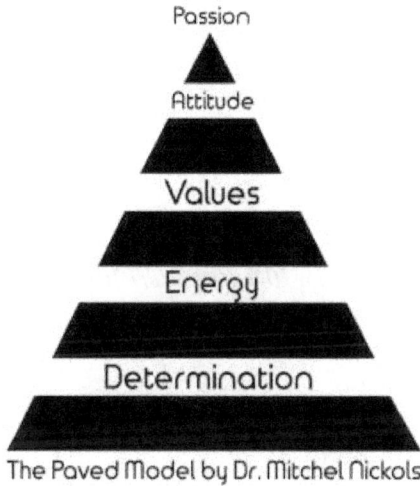

Passion

▲

Attitude

Values

Energy

Determination

The Paved Model by Dr. Mitchel Nickols

Through this model, passion can be identified as an anchor in difficult times. Attitude in a positive way can be the reference point even where others may not exhibit the same positive outlook. Where positive attitude is appreciated, it will increase productivity through inspiration. Values go to the core of what and why you do things on a regular basis. Energy is something that allows you to accelerate or decelerate according to the tasks at hand and the demand for successful completion. And determination reveals volition or strength that is required to goal-set and seek the best paths for winning again and again.

Every great dream begins with a dreamer. Always remember, you have within you the strength, the patience, and the passion to reach for the stars to change the world.

—Harriet Tubman

References

Barker, J. (2002). Video. The New Business of Paradigms. Burnsville, MN: Charthouse International Learning Corporation.

Bennis, W. (1994). On Becoming A Leader. Reading, MA: Addison-Wesley Publishing Company.

Buckingham, M. (2015). Stand Out 2.0: Assess Your Strengths, Find Your Edge, Win at Work. Brighton, MA: Harvard Business Review Press.

Chapman, S.W., & Rupured, M. (2016). Time Management: 10 strategies for better time management [PowerPoint]. Retrieved August 6, 2016, from The University of Georgia Cooperative Extension, www.wie.edu.

Cloud, H. (2013). Boundaries For Leaders. New York: Harper-Collins.

Collins, J. (2001). Good To Great. New York: HarperCollins.

Covey, S. (2013). The 7 Habits of Highly Effective People: Powerful Lessons in Personal Change. New York: Simon & Schuster.

Dalton, G., & Thompson, P. (1986). Novations: Strategies for Career Management. Glenview, Il: Scott, Foresman.

Daum, K. (2013). Define Your Personal Core Values: 5 Steps. Retrieved August 6, 2016, from http://www.inc.com/kevin-daum/define-your-personal-core-values-5-steps.html

Daum, K. (2013). 8 Things Really Successful People Do. Retrieved March 2, 2016, from http://www.inc.com/kevin-daum/8-things-really-successful-people-do.html

David. (2014, December). Carol Ryff's Model of Psychological Well-Being: The Six Criteria of Well-Being. Retrieved August 7, 2016, from http://livingmeanings.com/six-criteria-well-ryffs-multidimensional-model/

David. (2015, May). The Self-Determination Theory: Three ways towards Well-being. Retrieved August 7, 2016, from http://livingmenaings.com/three-needs-you-need-to-fulfill-for-Well-being/

David. (2015, June). Martin Seligman and his two theories of Happiness Authentic Happiness & PERMA. Retrieved August 7, 2016, from http://livingmeanings.com/martin-seligman-And-his-two-theories-of-happiness/

Deci, E. L., & Ryan, R. M. (2008). Self-Determination Theory: A Macrotheory of Human Motivation, Development, and Health. Canadian Psychology, 49 (3), 182-185.

Dewe, C. (2016). 11 Tips for Maintaining your Positive Attitude. Retrieved August 1, 2016, http://www.lifehack.org/articles/communication/11-tips-for-maintaining-your-positive-attittude.html

Editorial Team. (2016). Minimizing Distractions: 10 Ways to Take Control of Your Day. Retrieved from http://www.mindtools.com/pages/article/distractions.htm

Editorial Team. (2016). What Are Your Values? Retrieved from https://www.mindtools.com/pages/article/newTED_85. htm

Energy Is Everything//Creating A Personal Energy Management Profile. (2015). Retrieved August 6, 2016, from http:// www.onelittleminuteblog.com/2015/03/personal-energy-management /.

England, G.W. (1967). Personal value systems of American managers. Academy of Management Journal, 19, 53-68. Retrieved from http://dx.doi.org/10.2307/255244 .

Fabrega, M. (2016). 21 Ways to Create and Maintain a Positive Attitude. Retrieved August 1, 2016, from http:// daringtolivefully.com/positive-attitude

Fritz, R. (2008). The Power of a Positive Attitude: Discovering the Key to Success. New York: AMACOM.

George, B, Sims, P., McLean, A.N., & Mayer, D. (2007, March). Discovering Your Authentic Leadership. Harvard Business Review. Retrieved August 7, 2016, from hbr.org.

Goleman, D. (2006). Emotional Intelligence. New York: Bantam Publishing.

Gottschalk. M. (2013, April). 6 Ways to Build a More Positive Workplace. Retrieved March 27, 2016, from http:// money.usnews.com/money/blogs/outside-voices-careers/2013/04/29/6-ways-to-build-a-more-positive-workplace

Greenleaf, R., edited by Larry Spears (2002). Servant Leadership: A Journey into the Nature of Legitimate Power and Greatness. Mahwah: NJ: Paulist Press International.

Groysberg, B. & Abrahams, R. (2014, March). Manage Your Work, Manage Your Life. Harvard Business Review. Retrieved August 4, 2016, from https://hbr.org/2014/03/manage-your-work-manage-your-life.

Hereford, Z. Have a Personal Value System. Retrieved August 4, 2016, from http://www.essentiallifeskills.net/charactertraits.html

Hill, A. (1997). Just Business: Christian Ethics in the Marketplace. Downers Grove, Il: InterVarsity Press.

How to Be Determined. (2016). Retrieved March 27, 2016, from http://m.wikihow.com/Be-Determined.

Hudson, P. (2014). 10 Things That Truly Passionate People Do Differently. Retrieved August 13, 2016, from http://www.elitedaily.com

Huitt, W. (1999). Conation as an important factor of mind. Educational Psychology Initiative. Valdosta, GA: Valdosta State University. Retrieved April 20, 2016, from http://www.Edepsycinterative.org/topics/conation/conation.html

Ismail, H. (2016, March). Preferences in Business and Corporate Strategies: The Role of Personal Values. Contemporary Management Research, 12 (1), 25-46.

Johnson, C. E. (2001). Meeting the Ethical Challenges of Leadership: Casting Light or Shadow. Thousand Oaks, CA: Sage Publications.

Johnson, S. (1998). Who Moved My Cheese? New York: G.P. Putnam's Sons.

Jones, J. E., & Bearley, W. L. (2002). Managing Your Personal
Energy: Seventeen Ways to Avoid Burnout. Retrieved
August 5, 2016, from http://ous.iex.net/managing.htm

Juntilla, H. (2010). The 20 Essential Habits of Highly Passionate
People. Retrieved March 31, 2016, from http://www.
wakeupcloud.com/passionate-habits/

Kerpen, D. (2104, March). 15 Inspiring Quotes on Passion (Get
Back What You Love). Retrieved August 14, 2016, from
http://www.inc.com/dave-kerpen/15-quotes-on-
Passion-to-inspire-a-better-life.html

Kolbe, K. (1990). The conation connection. Reading, MA:
Addison-Wesley Publishing Company, Inc.

Lencioni, P. (2002). The Five Dysfunctions of a Team. San
Francisco: Jossey-Bass.

Loehr, A. (2014, May 6). How to Live with Purpose, Identify
Your Values and Improve Your Leadership. Retrieved from
http:www.huffingtonpost.com/anne-loehr/how-to-live-
purpose-_b_5187572.html

Maxwell, J. C. (2000). Failing Forward: Turning Mistakes into
Stepping Stones for Success. Nashville, TN: Thomas Nelson.

McKnight, W., & Chapman, E.N. (2010) Attitude: Protect Your
Most Precious Asset. Rochester, NY: Axzo Press.

Northouse, P. (2013). LEADERSHIP Theory and Practice (6th
Ed.). Los Angeles: Sage.

Oakley, E. & Krug, D. (1991). Enlightened Leadership: Getting
to the heart of change. New York: Simon & Schuster.

Palmer, I., Dunford, R., & Akin, G. (2009). Managing Organizational Change: A Multiple Perspectives Approach. New York: McGraw-Hill.

Pillay, S. (2011, November). How to Be Determined and Not Exhausted. Retrieved August 14, 2016, from m.huffpost.com

Pinder, C.C. (1998). Work Motivation in Organizational Behavior. Upper-Saddle River, NJ: Prentice-Hall.

Ray, L. (2016). The Effect of Employee Attitude on Productivity in the Workplace. Retrieved July 29, 2016, from http://www.oureverydaylife.com

Root, G. N. (2016). How Do Negative & Positive Attitudes Affect the Workplace? Retrieved August 1, 2016, from www.smallbusiness.chron.com

Rost, J. (1993). Leadership in the Twenty-First Century. Westport, Connecticut: Praeger.

Schein, E. (2009). The Corporate Culture Survival Guide. San Francisco: Jossey-Bass.

Schwartz, T. & McCarthy, C. (2007, October). Manage Your Energy, Not Your Time. Harvar Business Review. Retrieved August 6, 2016, from http://hbr.org/2007/10/manage-your-energy-manage-your-time.

Senge, P. (2006). The Fifth Discipline: The Art and Practice of the Learning Organization. New York: Doubleday.

Shnall, T. (2015). Five attitudes every leader must have to succeed! Retrieved July 30, 2016, from http://leadership hospitality.com

Size, D. (2016, June). Researchers Determine the Three Ways to Well-Being. Retrieved August 7, 2016, from http://www.huffingtonpost.com/david-sze/researchers-determine-the-threeways-to-well-being_b_7512510.html

Stanko, J. (1998). I Wrote This Book on Purpose...So You Can Know Yours. Mobile, Alabama: Evergreen Press.

Tej. (2012, November). What's The Point Of Living Average? Retrieved March 27, 2016, from From http://make-me-successful.com/deal-hard-times/

The Energy Project. (2014). Retrieved March 27, 2016, from https://theenergyproject.com/landing/sharedhumanera

Thygesen, T. (2016, January). Invest In Getting More Personal Energy: Easy Habits For The New Year. Retrieved from http://www.forbes.com/sites/tinethy-gesen/2016/01/02/invest-in-getting-more-personal-energy-8-habits/ #6fbe025058ca

Tracy, B. (2016). 7 Great Habits of the Most Successful People. Retrieved August, 2016, From http://www.briantracy.com/blog/personal-success-seven-good-habits-of-highly-Success-ful-people-goal-oriented/

Tucker, K. A. (2002, February). A Passion for Work. Retrieved March 27, 2016, from http://www.gallup.com/business journal/379/passion-work.aspx?version=print

Whitehurst, J. (2016, February). How to Build a Passionate Company. Retrieved July 3, 2016, from http://hbr.org/2016/02/how-tp-build-a-passionate-company

Williams, D. K. (2013). They Will Change Your Life: The 7 Non-Negotiables Of Winning. Retrieved August 7, 2016, from http://www.forbes.com/sites/davidkwilliams /2013/ 06/22/they-will…nge-your-life-the-7-non-negotiables-of-winning/#5d8890422102

Wolf, J., & Shelton, K. (2015). Seven Disciplines of a Leader: How to Help Your People, Team, and Organization Achieve Maximum Effectiveness. Hoboken, NJ: John Wiley & Sons.

Zenger, J.H., & Folkman, J.R. (2009). The Extraordinary Leader. New York: McGraw Hill.

Zenger, J.H., Folkman, J.R., Sherwin, R.H., & Steel, B. (2012). How To Be Exceptional: Drive Leadership Success By Magnifying Your Strengths. New York: McGraw Hill.

Zigarmi, D., Houson, D. Witt, D., & Diehl, J. (2011). Employee Work Passion. Retrieved March 21, 2016, from www.kenblanchard.com

About the Author

Dr. Mitchel A. Nickols, a sought after keynote, conference speaker and trainer, is a professional who relates well to diverse audiences: leadership development, team building, strategic planning, executive and administrative coaching, customer service, human services, business communications, board development, diversity and inclusion, etc.

Dr. Nickols holds a Ph.D. in Curriculum and Supervision and M. Ed., both from the University of Pittsburgh; Bachelor of Science in Education with minor equivalency in Communications, Sociology, Slippery Rock University; additional coursework at Pittsburgh Theological Seminary and Penn State University. As part of the faculty of Geneva College, Master of Science in Organizational Leadership, Human Services, Organizational Development, Human Resources, and Community Ministry, he developed curriculum for several courses. Some specific areas of teaching included History and Theory of Leadership, Leadership and Communications, Leadership and Ethics, Leadership and Motivation, Leadership and Decision Making, Leadership and Organizational Change, Strategic Planning, Organizational Dynamics, Generalist Practice-- Model & Theory, and The Church in its Community.

He is an adjunct professor at Point Park University in the Ed.D. Program, where he teaches doctoral students in Cultivating Ethical Diversity, and in Comparative Organizational Systems. Mitchel serves on the newly formed Point Park University Ed.D. Quality Advisory Board. Mitchel has mentored more than 400 professionals from nonprofit, for profit, and start-up organizations.

Mitchel has worked with school administrators and professional staff members over the years through administrative coaching, staff development, student retention and intervention strategies, parent groups, as well as keynote speaker for a number of school functions. His professional consulting work includes school districts, executives and managers, and board development. A 5-time national award-winning television producer and host, and an award-winning newspaper columnist, Mitchel is also a co-author of the published book titled "Leadership Essentials."